PIETER BRUEGHEL THE ELDER

PIETER BRUEGHEL THE ELDER
Detail from the engraving by Aegidius Sadeler, after Spranger

PIETER BRUEGHEL
THE ELDER

by

GUSTAV GLÜCK

With 40 colour plates
and 17 monochrome illustrations

LONDON: A. ZWEMMER LTD
MCMLI

Translated by Eveline Byam Shaw. The present edition
has been revised and brought up to date by the author.

Printed in Austria
Copyright 1951 by Anton Schroll & Co., Vienna
Colour blocks engraved by C. Angerer & Göschl, Vienna, Waterlow & Sons, Ltd., London (Plate 21),
Clichés Union S. A., Paris (Plate 37), Jean Malvaux, Brussels (Plate 17), Brend'amour, Simhart & Co.,
Munich (Pl. 10, 34, 41), Bendix & Lemke, Berlin (Pl. 15), F. Guhl & Co., Francfort on-the-Main (Pl. 38).
Printed by Christoph Reisser's Söhne, Vienna

Pieter Brueghel the Elder, or Peasant Brueghel, as he is sometimes called, is generally recognized today as one of the greatest and most original artists who ever lived; whether we understand and appreciate him fully is another question. His art is so powerful, so original, so many-sided that in order to understand it we have to consider many complicated problems. It well repays the closest study.

Brueghel's art is at the same time both ancient and modern; ancient, because it is so closely interwoven with the art and culture of earlier times; modern, because it is so completely new and astonishing and still appeals to us so powerfully that we are inclined to compare it with the production of our own days.

The range of his ideas embraces everything seen and thought of in his time: Earth, Heaven and Hell. Like most of his contemporaries, he was deeply religious and his religion plays an important part in his paintings. As opposed to the pious attitude of the fifteenth century which prevailed well into the sixteenth, we must admit that a more worldly and at the same time a more lively treatment of the subject is introduced.

In Brueghel's imagination, Bible subjects become intensely real; he sees the events of the Bible as scenes of exuberant peasant life. He prefers those aspects of the story that give him the opportunity of painting vast multitudes in continual movement. Only holy personages appear in a sort of idealized costume; the others wear contemporary dress, with here and there something more old-fashioned or fantastic. A contrast to scenes from the Bible is afforded by the sphere of ideas with which in those days the minds of men were scarcely less occupied: Death and the Devil.

The activities of hellish spirits, composed of the most diverse animal and human forms, the similar host of the Rebel Angels, the skeleton form of Death in all its horror, he depicts with the greatest impressiveness. The realm of classical Mythology occupies him less often. Allegory is dear to him and he loves to amplify it with illuminating scenes. He delights in the rendering of proverbs, proverbial sayings and parables. This gives him the opportunity of painting the World, topsy-turvy in his eyes, and, at the same time, according to religious ideas, the work of the Devil, the perverter.

Here, as in the pure genre pictures that evolve naturally from such subjects, he devotes himself entirely to the realistic aspect of life. Finally he pays homage to the greatness of Nature in landscapes which range from the simple " view " to atmospheric renderings of seasons of the year and the hours of the day.

The history of the master's life we know only in rough outline. Pieter Brueghel, who must have been born not long before 1530, came from the border territory somewhere between the modern Belgium and the modern Holland. It is not at all certain that Brueghel was the son of a peasant and spent his youth among peasants. At any rate one likes to believe that he received his spiritual upbringing in the neighbouring town of Bois-le-Duc and perhaps even received his first artistic incentive from the works of Hieronymus Bosch, his greatest predecessor, to be seen there in the churches.

It is not unlikely that his gifts for drawing and painting were discovered here and that his parents, relations or guardians had in mind one of the leading painters of the day to be his master. The choice fell on Pieter Coeck van Aelst, then generally accepted as the representative of official art. Educated in Italy, in close contact with the most learned circles of the day, himself a literary man, noted as a painter, architect and especially as draughtsman for festive decorations, tapestries and glass paintings, Pieter Coeck had received the distinction of Deacon of the Antwerp Guild of St. Luke and was Court-painter to the Emperor Charles V.

In 1551 Brueghel entered the Antwerp Guild of Painters as a Master and soon afterwards undertook a lengthy journey through France and Italy, which took him, as is well known, to Rome in the year 1553. Like Dürer, he brought home something new: the attainment of real freedom and nobility in his art as well as breadth in the conception of Nature which the contemplation of the Alps gave him.

At home, in Antwerp itself, he found a man exactly suited to publish his drawings and compositions as engravings. This was Hieronymus Cock, the first great publisher of engravings in the Netherlands. For him Brueghel executed a series of pen drawings as studies for engravings.

In the year 1563, Brueghel appears to have removed to Brussels where, in the same year, he married the daughter of his teacher Pieter Coeck, whom he had probably known from early childhood during his apprenticeship. In 1569 he died and was buried in the Church of Notre-Dame de la Chapelle, at Brussels. He left a widow with two boys of tender years who were both to make names for themselves as painters: Pieter Brueghel the Younger, also known as " Hell " Brueghel, and Jan Brueghel the Elder, known as " Velvet " Brueghel.

We should like to know more about Brueghel than is told in this short account of his career which does not differ fundamentally from the normal course of the life of an artist of his time; above all we should like to know what sort of being he was and something of his personality. We hear only that he was a quiet, sedate man who spoke little but loved to entertain his guests with practical jokes, frightening his friends and assistants with all kinds of apparitions and noise. That he was a man of the world, that he was not indifferent to the intellectual and probably also the religious tendencies of the day, is evident from his career, and still more from his work which is after all the best and most reliable source for the knowledge of his personality that we possess.

Brueghel—rather like Dürer and Holbein before him—was one of the great artists of a new age who lived in populous centres of commerce, had travelled and knew the world. They no longer depended for their artistic education only on the simple teaching of their Master and their school; their productions embraced far more, spiritually and artistically, than was the case in former times. The development of Brueghel's style, exemplified in his drawings and engravings, is not made much clearer to us by knowing that he was a pupil of Pieter Coeck. The stimulating effect on a

BIG FISHES EAT LITTLE ONES   Drawing, Vienna, Albertina

young artist of a big artistic publishing firm like that of Hieronymus Cock's in Antwerp, on the other hand, should not be underestimated.

But Brueghel had another interest in common with Hieronymus Cock—their fondness for the works of Hieronymus Bosch. Bosch died in the year 1516, that is to say certainly before Brueghel's birth, but most of the subjects of the younger artist's most remarkable productions, pictures of genre, proverbs, representations of hellish apparitions, the Devil and Death already occur in the work of Bosch. How near Brueghel sometimes came to Bosch is evident in the fact that one of the drawings of the year 1556, signed with Brueghel's name, was engraved and published by Hieronymus Cock as a work of Bosch. It is the drawing in the Albertina, *Big fishes eat little ones*, the subject of a widely known proverb, familiar to Shakespeare.

In such studies for engravings of which Brueghel drew a whole series for Hieronymus Cock soon after his return from his Italian journey and until the end of his life, he reverts unmistakably to the old fashioned style of Hieronymus Bosch, imitating in particular the fantastic forms of his phantoms while yet creating something entirely

7

DESIDIA (INDOLENCE) from the series of the Seven Deadly Sins   Drawing, Vienna, Albertina

new. It is only necessary to mention here, for example, the *Temptation of St. Anthony,* the *Last Judgment, Christ descending into Hell,* the two series of the *Seven Deadly Sins* and the *Seven Virtues.* These are not popular broadsheets, intended for the widest circulation, but profound intellectual works of art which with their pointed humour and their satire directed against the perversity of the World are intended for a small circle of scholars. In the sense of a thoroughly religious conception along with the belief in the Devil and Hell, upheld alike by Brueghel and his contemporaries, the folly of the World cannot be sufficiently disdained and mocked.

Naturally, Brueghel should not appear to us only as an incorrigible innovator: the spiritual and religious ideas and perceptions which he had at his disposal were based on the ideas of the Middle Ages. We meet with much of the material of Brueghel's art already in the pantomimes, ballets and pageants which were performed, in the fifteenth century, at the Courts of Burgundy, France and England. And something of the wisdom of the Court Fools of earlier times still runs in his blood as it does in Shakespeare's.

Hope from the series of the Seven Virtues   Drawing, Berlin, Print Room

So far we have only spoken of the world of ideas as it finds expression in Brueghel's studies for engravings which he began to execute soon after his journey to Italy. At the beginning of his career we know him chiefly as a draughtsman. The paintings which have made him famous all belong to the last decade of his evidently rather short life; he only began to sign and usually to date his pictures regularly from the year 1559 onwards. But undoubtedly he must have begun to paint sooner. To the earlier period of his career belong two large paintings with many figures: the *Adoration of the Magi* (Plate 6) and *Christ driving the Money Changers out of the Temple* (Plate 5).

Evidently, even before the year 1559 when, as has been already mentioned, Brueghel began as a general rule to date his pictures, he had already painted some easel pictures which, widely different in subject matter and treatment, already betray his individuality and his independence of foreign influences: the remarkable view of the *Harbour at Naples* (Plate 1), the vast *Landscape with Martyrdom of St. Catherine* (Plate 2), the very attractive picture of the *Archangel Michael*, in the collection of

9

Dr. A. F. Philips, at Eindhoven (Plate 3), the spacious *River Landscape with the peasant sowing,* of the year 1557 (Plate 7), and the extremely original *Landscape with the Fall of Icarus* (Plate 8). These pictures of the view of an Italian town, the saint, the single figure of the Archangel, the mythological subject, all bear evidence of the artist's residence in the south, and even in the landscape pictures Italian influence is to be recognized. But Brueghel appears to us first as a true Netherlander in the *Landscape with the Temptation of St. Anthony* (Plate 4), in which he contrasts the wonderful picture of Nature with the sorrows which the righteous must bear on earth.

After this period which lasted about eight years, from 1551 to 1558, comes the period of the masterpieces which begins with the year 1559 and lasts till the artist's death, that is to say, a full decade. The paintings of this period all show a perfect maturity of style, their artistic value is equal throughout and only continuity, not progress, is noticeable in their sequence. The colour is at first heavier, darker, gayer and stronger; gradually it becomes lighter and a preference is shown more for tender broken tones in combination with pure colours. The composition starts with a Gothic complexity, which is perceptibly simplified and finally achieves a perfect fusion of the narrative style with complete naturalism. The perspective from the first is clear and complete, later becomes less noticeable, and is finally achieved by imperceptible means as something that is taken for granted. The forms of human bodies no longer show the superficial observation to be seen in the early works, but presuppose a thorough study of Nature, to which many drawings bear witness. The contrast between the clumsy figures of profane characters and the slender, distinguished figures of saints becomes more apparent. In technique, preference is given to what we now call oil-painting, yet in the last period tempera paintings on canvas still occur, of which luckily two important examples are preserved in the Naples Museum (Plates 35 and 39).

When we consider the whole series of Brueghel's mature masterpieces from the point of view of narrative style it strikes one immediately that they differ entirely from the manner of all preceding early Netherlandish painting. Their style is far removed from the almost timid, pious tranquillity and solemnity of the great early masters as it is from the superficial and restless movement of their followers, who strove to imitate Italian beauty of form. And yet it has something in common with both of them; with the one in the faithful imitation of Nature, with the other in the more elaborate and flexible construction of the picture. In a certain sense, it exhibits a juxtaposition of the realistic and idealistic style. And in the forms of his idealistic figures with their over-long proportions and their exaggerated attitudes, Brueghel shows unmistakably the influence of Italian art.

The whole world is revealed to us in his paintings, the world not of course as it should be but as it is. Brueghel describes more than he teaches; he makes a statement without pronouncing judgment; he renders pure reality without criticism but seen with the incomparable eye of an artist. He is never instructive and the term "didactic"

LANDSCAPE WITH THE HOLY FAMILY   Drawing, Berlin, Print Room

applies to none of his paintings, however often it may have been used of them. On the other hand, he is no scoffer, but rather an observer, by no means indifferent to the emotions of life, to pain, strife, joy and mirth. But he himself neither weeps, laughs nor struggles. But a light, sorrowful smile may have sometimes lingered on his lips.

When he paints religious subjects, he wants to give us a picture of life, and with him this life becomes that of his own times. His fellow-countrymen appear in their usual dress as spectators, if not as active participants in the scene. A further characteristic of his art is that he rarely places the chief event of the story in the visible centre of the picture; he tries rather to conceal than to emphasize it. These points are already clearly demonstrated by his two paintings of Old Testament subjects: in the small picture of the *Death of Saul* (Plate 16), dated 1562, and in the large painting of the *Tower of Babel* (Plate 18), dated 1563. This is also true in principle of many of his paintings dealing with New Testament subjects: *Christ carrying the Cross* (Plate 19), dated 1564, *St. John the Baptist preaching Repentance* (Plate 30), dated 1566, the *Conversion of St. Paul* (Plate 33), dated 1567.

11

Brueghel's habit of concealing the real subject of a picture and letting it disappear in the surrounding masses may be explained by his opinion of the World, which he considered to be topsy-turvy and wrong-headed, blind to the importance even of the most momentous occurrences. Of course this point of view does not always hold good, and there are themes in the handling of which the artist sets himself a fresh problem each time. That of the *Adoration of the Magi,* which he represented in the early tempera painting (Plate 6) as a sort of state occasion with innumerable figures, he treats a second time simplified in a very remarkable composition (Plate 21), dated 1564, in which the spiritual significance surely lies in something else, in the slow-witted, uncomprehending astonishment of the spectators. Again, in a third representation of the subject, Brueghel conceives the scene of the *Adoration of the Magi* from quite another angle, as taking place in the snow (Plate 32, dated 1567).

Not only was he never disturbed by what we call today anachronism; it is the foundation of his own perfectly natural attitude to biblical subjects. We have seen—to cite a few examples—that he depicted Christ carrying the Cross as an execution, the Conversion of St. Paul as an army marching across the Alps. In the vivid representation and lively treatment of other New Testament subjects he goes a step further and sets those that take place at and near Christmas time in the wintry surroundings of his own home; such as the *Numbering of the People at Bethlehem* (Plate 28), dated 1566, and the *Massacre of the Holy Innocents* (Plate 29), and in the picture of the *Adoration of the Magi* (Plate 32) even a violent snowstorm rages. The subject of the *Flight into Egypt* (Plate 17), dated 1563, gives him the opportunity of painting an attractive spacious landscape meant to represent Egypt as he saw it in his dreams.

If the pictorial element predominates in Brueghel's mode of presenting almost all religious subjects, it occasionally happens that the master, who never repeats himself, produces a consistent, compact form of composition. Besides the upright picture of the *Adoration of the Magi,* the small grisaille painting of the *Death of the Virgin* (Plate 20) is to be mentioned.

To the spiritual ideas of Brueghel's day belonged also as a sort of counterpart, or reverse side, the representations of Hell, the Devil and Death. In the powerful painting of the *Triumph of Death* (Plate 12) he tells us of the inexorable power of Fate. If there the narrative, as it often is with Brueghel, is thoroughly disconnected and broken up by details, in the picture of the *Fall of the Rebel Angels* (Plate 14), of the year 1562, the representation of the battle of St. Michael and his Heavenly Hosts against the insect-like brood of Hell seems more consistent, compact and rounded off. Both styles of composition are combined in a certain sense in the painting of "*Mad Meg*" (Plate 13), of the year 1562 (?), in which, as Brueghel's only painted representation of Hell, his affinity with Hieronymus Bosch is clearly shown in the form of the various apparitions.

In his preference for proverbs and Bible parables, also, Brueghel comes into close relationship with Bosch. Although a moralising tendency seems to be far from Brueghel's

12

THE ALCHEMIST   Drawing, Berlin, Print Room

intention, accustomed as he is to accept things as they are, he yet prefers as subjects for his pictures proverbial sayings with a pessimistic foundation. In his superb picture of the *Proverbs* (Plate 10), dated 1559, within the frame of a sort of "Schildburgerdorf" (village of Schilda, the inhabitants of which have the same reputation as the Wise Men of Gotham), Brueghel combines a hundred separate scenes, representing all sorts of such well-known proverbial sayings. Their amalgamation gives a true picture of the perversity of the World. Brueghel retained his predilection for proverbs until the end of his life, and illustrated single proverbial sayings in several little pictures: in one, the sorrow for the *Faithlessness of the World* (Plate 35), of the year 1568; in another, the *Proverb of the Bird's Nest* (Plate 36), also 1568; in another, the *Merry Way to the Gallows* (Plate 38), also of the year 1568; and finally in a fourth, a stormy turbulent *Seascape*, a whale playing with a barrel instead of following the ship, suggesting the simile of a man who for the sake of trivialities misses his true advantage (Plate 44).

To the same range of ideas of the perversity of the World belongs Brueghel's only representation of a subject taken from folklore: the *Fool's Paradise* (Plate 34), dated 1567. He appears even greater in the illustration of Bible parables. Two superlative

13

River Landscape with Rocks   Drawing, Berlin, Print Room

pictures are examples of this: the *Unfaithful Shepherd* (Plate 40) who has left the flock entrusted to his charge to the ravages of the wolf, and the *Parable of the Blind* (Plate 39), dated 1568, in which a straggling chain of six tragic figures, linked together, approach their irrevocable fate, the headlong fall into the ditch. These are fundamentally allegories, the meaning of which is already given in the Gospel, but which here attain to an intensity of expression never before or since achieved in pictorial art. In a picture of much earlier date, Brueghel treated an essentially different and purely profane form of allegory, the *Battle between Carnival and Lent* (Plate 9), dated 1559. Here he surrounds the symmetrical arrangement of the chief scene of the battle between Carnival and Lent with numerous popular scenes, as in the picture of the *Proverbs* (Plate 10), and in a third picture, that of the *Children's Games* (Plate 11).

If in the paintings already mentioned the human form, as rendered by Brueghel, ranges from idealized figures to realistically treated cripples and blind men, he also rules supreme in another province that is quite his own, which certainly plays no such

14

Shooting Hares   Original Etching

part as one would imagine from his nickname "Peasant Brueghel", but yet comprises some of his greatest achievements: that of the genre picture, the peasant subject. Here Brueghel appears no longer as a story-teller, but as an illustrator.

His peasants believe themselves to be unobserved by the spectator and lead their own life quite unselfconsciously. In the earliest of these pictures crowded with figures he does not fully attain the truth to life and nature of his later peasant subjects. The single heads and figures, types and expressions, do not yet show the individuality and realism of his more mature period. But now, coinciding with the first of his masterpieces, he begins an extremely penetrating and careful study of life. He makes pen-drawings of the most diverse peasant types, men and women, and notes with precision on the same sheet the colours of the clothes, notes which could only be intended for himself, the painter, and not for the spectator or purchaser.

Usually he himself remarks that these drawings are done from life (« naert het leven »). These sheets of studies are not hasty, chance sketches but represent methodically

15

SPRING   Drawing, Vienna, Albertina

executed work which in its truth to and respect for Nature is comparable to the learned precision of an ethnographer.

The splendid composition of the *Wedding Dance* (Plate 27), of the year 1566, is a development from earlier attempts at the same subject. The rendering of the peasant life in a picture of a very similar subject, the *Dance of the Peasants* (Plate 43), is even more powerful and irresistible in effect. The same is true of a second picture, usually thought of as a companion piece to the *Dance of the Peasants* the *Peasants' Wedding* (Plate 42).

Brueghel is not indifferent to the shady side of life and even devotes a little panel (Plate 37) to the *Cripples*. Apart from a single portrait of animals, the charming little picture of *Two Monkeys* (Plate 15), all the animals which occur in his pictures are derived purely from memory. They are true to life in their movements, but drawn entirely from memory; they are ordinary animals of common breed suited to the country people.

16

SUMMER   Drawing, Hamburg, Kunsthalle

And finally what shall one say of Brueghel's pictures of unfrequented Nature, of his landscape paintings? Words fail to describe them in all their grandeur. If he only gradually attains complete coherence of design in his figure compositions, it seems to be a foregone conclusion in his rendering of Nature; he is the born landscape painter. And in fact he begins his artistic career, as far as we can see, with landscape drawings. Pure landscape in the modern sense of the term was in those days almost a novelty.

Here, too, then as in so many other aspects of his art, he is not exactly the independent innovator he may easily appear to us to be on account of the grandeur and irresistible power of his art. But we may attribute this grandeur to his intimate love and understanding of Nature which, even in the landscapes which he almost always introduced into his figure compositions, are so impressively realistic that his figures seem to live and have grown up quite naturally in their surroundings.

Among the Master's actual landscapes, the two paintings: the view of the *Harbour at Naples* (Plate 1), the *Landscape with Martyrdom of St. Catherine* (Plate 2), and

17

PAIR OF DRAUGHT=HORSES   Drawing, Vienna, Albertina

the *River Landscape with the peasant sowing* (Plate 7), mark the earlier stages of his development. His landscape with the *Flight into Egypt* (Plate 17) and especially the five pictures of the Months which obviously form part of a series, are among Brueghel's most masterly productions. What remains of them is of the highest artistic and historical importance. The infinitely varied atmospheric effects of the different seasons of the year have never before been expressed in so convincing, so ravishing and captivating a way; never before has so complete a picture of the whole of Nature been conceived; never before have the figures been so perfectly in harmony with their surroundings, that they seem to be a part of Nature itself.

The series begins with the *Hunters in the Snow* (Plate 22), dated 1565, probably intended to represent the month of February. With it, Brueghel became the founder of a wide-spread class of Netherlandish painting, the winter picture. He himself, as we have seen, placed many of his Bible subjects in a setting of snow, and besides this picture belonging to the series of the Months, he painted yet another little *Winter Landscape* of the greatest charm (Plate 31), of the same year, 1565.

18

STUDIES FROM LIFE   Drawing, Vienna, collection of Prince Liechtenstein

The remaining subjects from the series of the Months show that he was able to interpret the atmosphere of other seasons of the year with no less feeling for their essential, typical quality. In the *Stormy Day* (Plate 23), dated 1565, which probably stands for the month of March, he depicts the forboding atmosphere of earliest spring; in the *Hay Harvest* (Plate 24), representing June, late spring or early summer; in the *Corn Harvest* (Plate 25), dated 1565, probably the month of July, he renders the stifling effect of midsummer heat; in the *Return of the Herd* (Plate 26), dated 1565, presumedly November, he renders a cold day of late Autumn.

To these superb pictures of atmospheric effects, unequalled in the whole History of Art, is to be added the small *Seascape* (Plate 44) which, although it has the pretext of illustrating a proverbial saying, may be considered as the first perfect example of Netherlandish marine painting. How far has Brueghel travelled in the art of landscape painting from the fine, almost miniature-like rendering of the waves in the early picture of the *Harbour at Naples* (Plate 1) to the broad, flowing treatment of the huge waves, lashed by storm, in this late work.

19

ARTIST AND CONNOISSEUR   Drawing, Vienna, Albertina

It is especially the class of art in which subject interest is subordinated to purely pictorial effect, the genre picture and the landscape, that, in the further development of modern painting, has been most decidedly influenced by Brueghel's work. Without ever surpassing him, the artists of the seventeenth century took Brueghel as their model and, following his lead, developed their various branches of painting. The peasant subject of Adriaen Brouwer is hardly conceivable without him, and even so many-sided and inspired an artist as Rubens owes much to him.

Among the succeeding influences of the eighteenth and nineteenth century, so far removed in spirit from Brueghel's peculiar genius, his art, his name even, sank almost into oblivion. His way of seeing things, simply, without pose or rhetoric, his spiritual, reflective, contemplative attitude to the world and mankind, his wonderful gift for painting, his fine sense of colour, his simplified construction of form in two dimensions, the value of the enchanting, atmospheric quality of his landscape have received full recognition again only in our own day.

There is in fact hardly one among all artists of the past who appeals so much to us moderns as Brueghel, in form and colour, who gives us as much as he does, in his conception of the World and of Nature, of his whole mentality. That he should touch our feelings, nay, our hearts so nearly, may be due to circumstances; for he too lived in a period of upheaval and changing values, and gave expression in his art, prophetically, to much that we feel today. But that which he really lived for, the incomparable achievement of his work, is valid not merely for his time nor for ours, but so long as the greatness of creative power in art is appreciated.

PLATES

1.

THE HARBOUR AT NAPLES
Rome, Doria Gallery

On panel. 16 by 27$^1/_2$ inches. Unsigned, but rightly
recognized as Brueghel's by Ludwig Burchard on account of the similarity of the composition with the engraving of 1561 by Frans Huys, after Brueghel's *Battle
of Messina.*

This comparatively small picture might almost be considered a forerunner of later Netherlandish marine
painting, although the setting is of course Italian. Ships
and the sea were favourite subjects with Brueghel, to
which he often returned. This is shown not only by the
series of 13 variations of ships engraved after Brueghel
by Frans Huys, but also by the fact that two paintings
of similar subjects are recorded in the Granvella Collection at Besançon and among Rubens' effects at his
death. Whether the picture in question is to be identified
with one of those it is impossible to say for certain.

2.

LANDSCAPE WITH
MARTYRDOM OF ST. CATHERINE
New York, Private Collection

On panel. 24 by 46¹/₂ inches. Unsigned. First published by Edouard Michel, and later, after it had undergone a cleaning, recognized by Max J. Friedländer and myself as Brueghel's and placed among the master's early works.

The subject of the martyrdom of St. Catherine occurs in Netherlandish illuminated manuscripts of the fifteenth century and was also used by Albert Dürer in an early woodcut. Joachim de Patinir was the first to place it in a spacious landscape, as in a small picture in the Vienna Gallery, and in a large painting on canvas which was in the collection of the noted art-lover, Cardinal Grimani at Venice in 1521, but has been lost since. It remains doubtful whether Brueghel had seen this painting and whether it suggested to him the picture under consideration. At any rate, it is the landscape that is made of chief importance, even more so than in Patinir's treatment of the subject, and, by relegating the execution in the background, Brueghel almost seems to conceal the real subject, as was his habit in his later works. The charm of his picture is indeed afforded chiefly by the representation of nature, livened only by a few genre figures, and the wide outlook towards hills, rocks, the sea, and the cloudy sky. It is in the details of the landscape and of the small figures that this work agrees most convincingly in style with the drawings and paintings that Brueghel had done in Italy. This is corroborated by the present owner's statement according to which this picture, which is now on plywood, was originally on poplar wood. As poplar wood was then in general use in Italy, this seems to confirm that the picture had been painted during Brueghel's Italian journey, not later than 1553.

3.

THE ARCHANGEL MICHAEL
Eindhoven, Collection of Dr. A. F. Philips

On panel. 17 by 11½ inches. Unsigned. First published as a work of Brueghel by P. Wescher.

The intention of the picture is, probably, to suggest that St. Michael, leaving to his companions the task of over-powering the followers of Satan in Heaven, has himself descended to Earth to fight and vanquish the Devil in his own domain. The heavenly beauty of the landscape affords a striking contrast, evidently quite intentional, to the moral depravity and perversity of the World. Brueghel here challenges comparison in a certain sense with a much later thinker, Chamfort, to whom the physical world appeared as the work of a good and powerful Being who had been obliged to leave part of his design to be carried out by an evil Being, while he considered the moral world to be the creation of a Devil gone mad.

4.

LANDSCAPE WITH THE TEMPTATION OF ST. ANTHONY
London, Robert Frank Collection

On panel. 22³/₄ by 33¹/₂ inches. In 1934 it was discovered in the possession of an old Belgian family and was first published by Leo van Puyvelde.

The preference for the subject of the temptation of St. Anthony appears early in the history of Netherlandish art, and is probably based on the fundamental idea, first expressed in the Psalms: "The righteous must suffer, but the Lord helpeth him in all things". The Gothic love of the droll and grotesque is also well suited by the subject. The masterpiece of this kind is the famous hinged altarpiece by Hieronymus Bosch, today in the Lisbon Museum, a masterpiece of sensitive painting and colour, which was much admired in the first half of the sixteenth century and was copied and imitated over and over again. Brueghel treated the subject in his drawing for the engraving of the year 1556 and closely followed his predecessor in the fantastic rendering of hellish apparitions, composed of human and animal bodies or parts of bodies, and even of all sorts of other objects, so that the figure of the Saint seems almost of secondary importance. In the picture under discussion, in a similar way, the emphasis is on the landscape, and it is divine Nature that is made of chief importance, even more than in the picture of the *Archangel Michael* (Plate 3). The principal figure, St. Anthony, certainly appears twice, without however being in the least conspicuous—a concealment of the real subject which is thoroughly characteristic of Brueghel. On the one hand, we see the Saint withdrawn into quiet seclusion near the wood, in the dark of the hermit's cave in the rocks, roofed in with rough-hewn boards, beset by only a few apparitions; on the other, we see him in the air riding on a flying fish, mercilessly tormented by beings half-devil, half-animal. The numerous other scenes of grotesque fantasy that are to be discerned in this beautiful landscape literally baffle description;—we can no more explain it all in detail than we can interpret the hellish apparitions in the works of Bosch.

The advanced style of the landscape and the essentially deep, strong colour scheme suggest a date about 1558 for this picture.

5.

CHRIST DRIVING THE MONEY CHANGERS
OUT OF THE TEMPLE
Copenhagen, Statens Museum

On panel. 40 by $61^1{}_2$ inches. Unsigned. Not in the best condition. Recognized and published as a work of Brueghel by M. J. Friedländer.

The subject is adapted very freely from the account in the Gospel and the traders' profanation of the holy precincts is illustrated in a particularly drastic way. From the open hall of the Temple, on the round altar of which are two statues—one of them, no doubt, Moses with the tables of the law — Jesus is driving out the buyers and sellers, among them the money changers, with their bags of money and their tables. On the right, they are streaming out of the Temple past the statue of an idol with their animals and their bags; on the left, a charlatan is plying his trade; behind him appears a man in the pillory (perhaps the Jester in the pillory who appears elsewhere in Brueghel's work, cf. Plate 10, No. 62); in the centre, the halt and maimed are begging for alms. In the distance, on the right, is the procession to Calvary, which might be interpreted as an ironic antitype to the driving out of the money changers, or even as the retaliation and vengeance of the ignoble world. On the wall to the left is a strange clock, which with a pointer in the form of a human arm indicates the hour of midnight; a motive that we meet again in Brueghel's rendering of *Desidia* (Indolence), reproduced on page 8, from the series of the Seven Deadly Sins. A similar clock occurs in his *Triumph of Death* (Plate 12).

6.

THE ADORATION OF THE MAGI
(IN TEMPERA)
Brussels, Royal Museum

Tempera on canvas. 45$^1/_2$ by 64 inches. Unsigned. Has suffered from damp.

Brueghel was to treat this subject again in two entirely different ways (see Plates 21 and 32). The composition under consideration is without doubt the earliest version. Nowhere in Netherlandish painting, before this date, not even in the Triptych of Hieronymus Bosch in the Prado at Madrid, is such emphasis laid on the striking contrast between the riches of the Three Holy Kings with their innumerable retinue and the poverty of the birthplace and surroundings of the Saviour. Even the seventeenth century can show no composition of the same subject more crowded with figures.

7.

RIVER LANDSCAPE
WITH THE PEASANT SOWING
Antwerp, Collection of F. Stuyck del Bruyère

On panel. 29 by 40 inches. Signed lower right:
BRVEGHEL 1557 (the first two letters of the name
and the first figure of the date are rubbed).
Not in the best condition. First mentioned by Max J. Friedländer as a "Landscape painting, which in construction
and feeling is comparable to the drawings of mountain
scenery, interpreted by Tolnai in the book on Brueghel
with such extreme penetration". The correspondence with
the series of large landscape engravings seems to me even
closer than that with Brueghel's drawings. The motive of
birds pecking up the seeds as soon as they are sown by
the Peasant is an excellent example of the artist's conception of the perversity and uselessness of human activities.

8.

LANDSCAPE WITH THE FALL OF ICARUS
Brussels, Royal Museum

Tempera (apparently partly worked over in an oil technique) on canvas. 29 by 44 inches. Unsigned.

The representation of the subject follows Ovid's story in the "Metamorphoses" very closely. Even the characters of lesser importance mentioned by Ovid, the ploughman, fisherman and shepherd, are not lacking. The motive of the peasant with the plough is given added significance by Brueghel by the introduction of the corpse of an old man lying in the bushes on the left. The meaning of this is made clearer by the German proverb: "Es bleibt kein Pflug stehen um eines Menschen willen, der stirbt" (No plough comes to a standstill because a man dies). The figure of Icarus fallen headlong into the sea, with only his legs showing above the water in the middle distance on the right, is a very meagre indication of the main subject, in contrast to the detailed treatment of the genre figures and the beautiful landscape. It is remarkable that in the picture under consideration the figure of Daedalus flying through the air is entirely absent and that the sun, as though it were evening, appears just above the horizon, whereas, according to Ovid's story, it should be high overhead in order to be strong enough to melt the wax of Icarus' wings. In another example of the same composition, which I believe to be original (at the time of writing in the possession of the Galerie J. Herbrand in Paris), the figure of Daedalus hovering in the air is retained, and the sun, which in this case is imagined to be high up in the sky and does not come into the picture at all, directs its destructive rays upon Icarus, so that some feathers which he has lost in his fall come fluttering downwards. This version seems to me to represent Brueghel's original conception of the subject. The archaic style of the composition permits us to date it soon after the artist's journey to Italy, about 1554—1558.

For the interpretation of the subject, we may compare a passage in Sebastian Brant's "Ship of Fools":

"Hett Phaeton syn farren gelon   (Had Phaeton kept to his course
Vnd Icarus gemåcher gton,   And Icarus less rashly flown,
Vnd beid gfolgt jrs vatters rott,   Had they obeyed their fathers' lores,
Sie wern nit jn der jugent dott."   A longer life they would have known.)

THE BATTLE BETWEEN CARNIVAL AND LENT
Vienna, Kunsthistorisches Museum

On panel. 46 1/2 by 64 1/2 inches. Signed lower left: BRVEGEL 1559.

The remarkable conception of this picture is not entirely due to Brueghel, original as is his treatment of the theme, but goes back to older traditions. Among the Netherlandish pictures on canvas in the possession of the Medici family in Florence in the 15th century, was one with the allegoric figure of Lent, mocked by figures drinking and feasting. In the possession of the Spanish court in the Hunting Box at Pardo there was a large picture of *Carnival and Lent* by Hieronymus Bosch, the composition of which is still preserved, apparently, in a long grisaille picture, in the collection of Baron Thyssen.

Brueghel resembles his predecessors in subject only. While Bosch limits himself to comparatively few figures and divides the opposing parties by means of groups of dancers, Brueghel gives us a regular picture of the world and illustrates this battle between Carnival and Lent with the greatest clearness and with countless illuminating episodes. Prince Carnival, a corpulent fellow, bestrides a large wine-cask, with a pie as headdress, and for weapons a long spit with a pig's head and other delicacies. His opponent is an embodiment of Lent, a lean old hag with a bee-hive as headdress and a long-handled wooden shovel, on which are two herrings; her chair is placed on a wheeled platform and she is drawn along by a monk and a nun. On either side are seen their followers, here occupied with the rich, hearty fare of Carnival time, there with the sparing, frugal nourishment of Lent. The scenes of the middle and further distance are divided in the same way, the gay, motley doings of Carnival are shown on the left, the quiet contemplative life of Lent on the right. The companions of the figure of Carnival wear masks and fantastic dresses. Among the innumerable people who throng the streets and squares, are seen couples who dance in a chain, a procession led by a bagpipe player, a gaily-dressed fool with a torch, cripples, a waffle-baker, and so on. Two Carnival plays are being performed out-of-doors: in front of the inn at the sign of the "Blue Ship", in the foreground on the left, a play of the "Ugly Bride", generally thought to be "The Marriage of Mopsus and Nisa" (a motive taken from Virgil's Eclogues), and in front of the inn at the sign of the "Dragon", in the background further away, the story of "Valentine and Orson", still known today as an English fairy tale. The right half of the picture tells quite a different story. Even the dresses here are darker and less gaily-coloured. The people are streaming in and out of church, some of them carrying prayer-stools. A baker's shop, and a fish market, and instead of the wine-casks and beer-mugs a well of water, are signs of the simplified fare. Now too is the time for works of mercy: the cripples who in the left part of the picture passed unnoticed are refreshed and given alms among other poor people. Groups of playing children strike a lively note on both sides of the picture.

10.
THE NETHERLANDISH PROVERBS
Berlin, Kaiser Friedrich-Museum

On panel. 46 by 64 $^1/_8$ inches. Signed lower right: BRVEGEL 1559.
The sign of the inn on the left, a globe with a cross pointing down instead of up, indicates the meaning of this picture: it is the World Turned Upside Down, shown in many little scenes illustrating the foolishness of mankind. Brueghel's interpretations of the proverbs and sayings are spread over the buildings and the streets of an imaginary village. "The apparent disorder of the plan of the village", says Wilhelm Fraenger, "does not strike one as in the least disturbing. We accept it in good faith and abandon ourselves to the mystery of the place with that bewildered wonder and curiosity in which we are accustomed to wander through the romantic streets of dream cities." The various episodes all take place simultaneously side by side, but entirely independently of one another, just as might happen by chance in real life. The explanations of proverbs, sayings, and similes, which we give here in translation, are based upon a revision of W. Fraenger's that was placed at our disposal by Mr. Jan Borms of Voorburg near the Hague. The numbers correspond to those on the fly-leaf of our reproduction:

1 Would you thatch your house with tarts?
2 Marriage under the broom
3 He hangs out the broom (i. e. his wife is absent)
4 He has it at his fingers' ends
4a His knife is hanging down from the window (a challenge)
4b To go about in wooden shoes (i. e. to be kept waiting. We say, to cool one's heels)
5 They lead each other by the nose
6 A fool is making the cards
6a It is on the cards
6b The die is cast
7 He sh—s upon the world
7a The world turned upside down
8 To let it go through the handle of the scissors (i. e. to overlook a fault)
9 Leave one egg in the nest
10 He p—s on the moon
11 He has an aching tooth at someone
11a }
11b } Better a clout than a hole out
11c Roofs have rafters (we say, walls have ears)
12 Here you may poke your nose into other people's pot
13 The fool got a trimming
13a It grows out of the window (i. e. it is an open secret)
14 Two faces under one hood
15 To shoot one arrow after another (i. e. to throw good money after bad)
16 She would bind the devil himself to a cushion
17 A hypocrite (He is biting the pillar of a church, as the Dutch have it)
18 She carries fire in one hand and water in the other
19 His herring will not roast here
20 Every herring must hang by his own gill
21 To fall to the ground between two stools
21a Smoke cannot harm iron
21b The spindles have fallen into the ashes (i. e. our hopes have turned to dust and ashes)
22 At open doors dogs come in
23 Here the sow pulls out the bung (this means bad husbandry)
24 To run one's head against a wall
25 Give not a naked sword in a madman's hand (In a cuirass means mad with rage)
26 Who shall bell the cat?
27 He is armed to his teeth
28 An iron-eater (we say, a fire-eater)
29 Do not count your eggs before they are laid (or, your chickens before they are hatched)
30 He gnaws on one bone only
31 That is where the scissors hang out (This is said of a cut-purse)

32 He is double-mouthed (i. e. double tongued)
33 Here's a great cry, and little wool, as the fellow said when he sheared his hogs (we say, much ado about nothing)
33a 'Tis ill shaving against the wool
33b Shear sheep that have them
33c Patient as a lamb
34 One holds the distaff and the other spins (i. e. they carry the gossip around)
35 To burn daylight, or, to carry a basketful of light outdoors ("To carry coals to Newcastle")
36 One must sometimes hold a candle to the devil
37 It is foolish to make the devil one's confessor
38 He breathes it into his ear (scandal-mongering)
39 The crane treats the fox to a dinner
39a What is the good of a nice dish if it is empty?
39b A skimmer
39c It is chalked up
40 When the calf is drowned, you fill the ditch in (or, When the steed is stolen, you shut the stable door)
41 The world twirls on his thumb
42 To put a spoke in a person's wheel
43 In the world one must bend not to break
44 He would even beard the Lord
45 To throw roses before swine
46 She hangs a blue cape round him (i. e. she is unfaithful to him)
47 To have the pig's skin one must kill it
48 Two dogs at one bone can't get together
49 He sits on red-hot coals (i. e. he is on tenterhooks)
50 He p—s the other fellow's fire out
50a The joint will never roast before such a small fire
51 He knows how to land his fish
52 He falls through the basket (This saying refers to a well-known farce, in which a refused suitor falls through a basket)
53 He is kept in suspense
54 To catch the hen's egg she lets the goose's egg go
55 No gaping against the oven
56 He cannot have both cakes (Who hunts two hares, leaves the one, and loses the other)
57 He is a lazy worker who always looks for his tools
57a Hatchet and helve (i. e. something whole and useful)
57b A hoe without a handle (i. e. something useless)
58 It's no good crying over spilt milk

59 The last couple pulls for the cake (a biscuit in B shape is used in this pastime)
59a He clings to a tree
61 He sits in his own light
62 He fiddles in the stocks
63 Better ride an ass that carries me than an ox that throws me
64 'Tis one beggar's woe to see another by the door go
64a He can see through an inch board if there is a hole in it
65 He rubs his back against the door
66 Kissing the door-knob (a formal act of submission)
67 It is ill fishing before the net
68 Big fishes swallow up the little ones
69 He is angry because the sun shines on the water
70 He throws his money into the river
71 They sh— through the same hole (some say, they p— in the same quill)
71a It is like a sh—house hanging over a ditch
72 He kills two flies with one flap
73 She watches the stork (i. e. she is idle)
73a Fine feathers make fine birds
74 He turns his coat according to the wind (some say, pull down your hat on the wind side)
75 Words and feathers are tossed by the wind
76 He cuts large thongs of another man's leather
77 The pitcher that goes often to the well comes home broken at last
78 Who takes an eel by the tail and a woman by her word may say that he holds nothing
79 It is hard to swim against the stream
80 He left his cowl on the fence (i. e. he is a runaway monk)
81 He sees dancing bears (he is very hungry)
82 He is on fire
83 The hogs run into the wheat (i. e. everything goes wrong)
84 He set my house on fire only to roast his eggs
84a The back door robs the house
85 As the wind blows you must set your sail
86 He is sailing dead against the eye of the wind
87 He wonders why the geese go barefoot
88 Horse dung is no figs (some say, all is not butter the cows sh—)
88a He pulls the log (i. e. he is crazily in love but not loved in return)
89 Fear makes the old wife trot
90 He cheats the gallows
91 Where the carcase is the crows will gather
92 If the blind lead the blind . . .
92a Don't say you have reached the town when you see the tower from afar

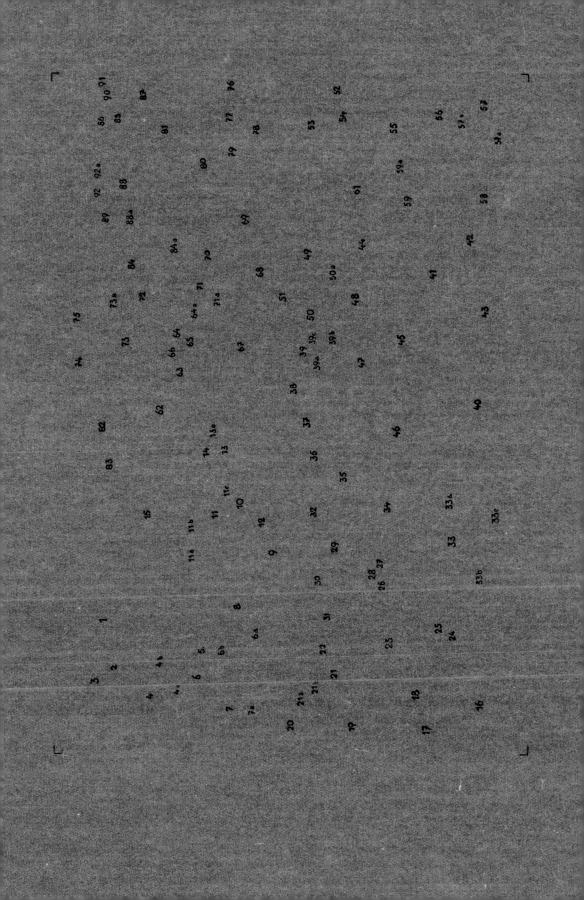

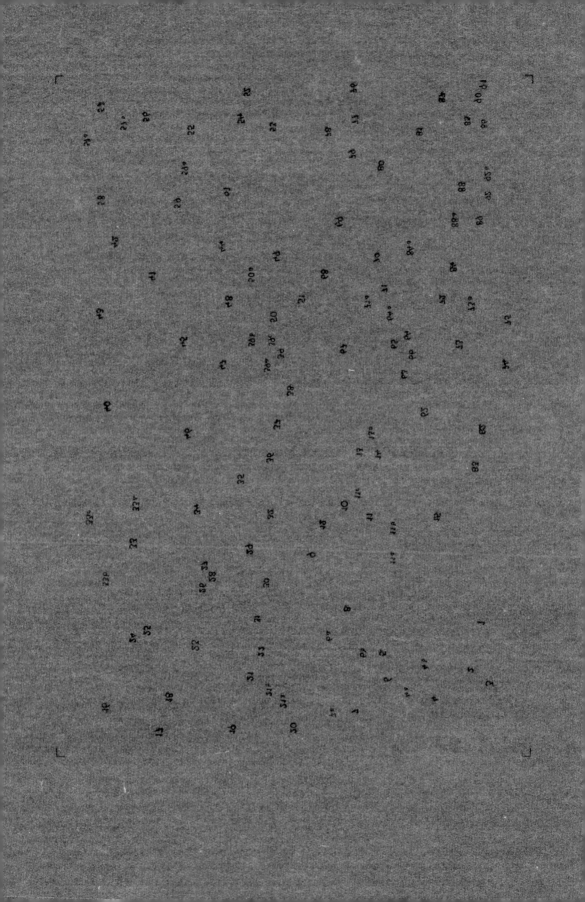

11.

CHILDREN'S GAMES
Vienna, Kunsthistorisches Museum

On panel. $45\,^1/_4$ by $63\,^1/_2$ inches. Signed lower right:
BRVEGEL 1560.

A whole town is given up to the children for their amusements, not a grown-up person is to be seen. The games are probably the same as those still played today and therefore need no explanation. Boys and girls play with hobby-horses, tops, hoops of various kinds, with masks, amuse themselves with leap-frog, walking on stilts, pickaback and swinging, Blind Man's Buff, standing on their heads, riding, climbing trees, bathing. Girls play at a wedding and with a dolls' house.

In the picture of the *Battle between Carnival and Lent* children play quite a prominent part, which may perhaps have suggested to Brueghel the idea of letting them appear for once quite by themselves. On the other hand, as Dr. Erica Tietze-Conrat has pointed out, he may have meant the subject to represent one of the Ages of Man, Childhood (Infantia), as the first of a series of paintings, the number of which it is impossible to determine, the Ages of Man, according to different authorities, varying from two to twelve. It would be easier to take a number somewhere in the middle, for instance seven, in which Shakespeare's melancholy Jaques divides the world in "As you like it".

12.

THE TRIUMPH OF DEATH
Madrid, Prado

On panel. 46 by 63$^3/_4$ inches. Unsigned. Painted about 1561—1562. From the popularity of the Dance of Death in the Middle Ages we can realize the immense importance of the conception of Death and his Skeleton form in pictorial art. With Brueghel the idea has developed into an army of skeletons rather like the Angel host of St. Michael or Satan's army of Devils. In a vast barren landscape with bare hills, leafless trees, stagnant pools of water, ruined or burning buildings, with a view of further conflagrations in the distance and a mournful sea, innumerable skeletons are at work, accompanied by the clanging of a bell, tolled by two skeletons, a fanfare of trumpets blown by skeletons in shrouds, and two kettle-drums beaten by another skeleton. In a clock fixed up on the wall of a building on the left, yet another skeleton serves as a finger and, as is shown in later replicas, clearly points to the hour of midnight. With arrows, scythes, hatchets, millstones, even with nets, some singly, some in dense bands, the skeletons wage war on helpless mankind, among whom are those of all ranks: a king, a cardinal (it is remarkable that he wears a blue mantle), monks, knights, noblemen, lansquenets, soldiers, bourgeoisie and peasants. Many flee, or, in desperation take to arms. A fool creeps under a table, a party of ladies and gentlemen are surprised at a feast, a couple making music are accompanied on the fiddle by a skeleton. Thieves are hanging on the gallows, broken on the wheel or beheaded; crows are hovering round. A wagon piled high with skulls is being driven along. Around a chapel by the sea-shore there is a crowd of mourners. A ship sinks in the obviously calm sea.

13.

MAD MEG («DULLE GRIET»)
Antwerp, Musée Mayer van den Bergh

On panel. 45 $\frac{1}{4}$ by 63 $\frac{1}{2}$ inches. The artist's signature has been daubed over in an old restoration and rendered completely illegible. We believe the date may be read M · D · LXII.

This picture is still closely related to the range of ideas of Hieronymus Bosch from whose hand there is the picture of a witch, now in a Spanish collection. The expression «Dulle Griet» (Mad Margaret) corresponds with Megaera or Xanthippe and means a kind of female Hell-fiend. It is remarkable that the barrel of a cannon of the time of Philip the Good, in the Friday Market at Ghent, bears this name to this day, while Scottish and Irish cannon are called by the names of "Mad Meg" and "Roaring Meg". The description of the picture in an old inventory as "furia" has some bearing on this point, for Megaera was certainly one of the furies. It is the same evil woman who is able to bind the Devil himself to a cushion, a subject represented in Brueghel's picture of the *Proverbs* (Plate 10, No. 16). Here she appears in Hell with a wild look, screaming with open mouth, warlike and armed with helmet, cuirass, sword and kitchen knife, carrying her spoils, among them a casket of gold, on her arm, under her arm and in her apron. At the same time she is the leader of a great band of women who, in the thickest of the fight, know how to come to terms even with the Devils of Hell. Max J. Friedländer aptly reminds us of German proverbs such as: "Einen Raubzug tun an der Höllenpforte" (To raid Hell) or "Mit dem Degen in der Faust in die Hölle gehen" (To go to Hell with sword in hand).

14.

THE FALL OF THE REBEL ANGELS
Brussels, Royal Museum

On panel. 46 by 63³/₄ inches. Signed lower left: M · D · LXII · BRVEGEL.

The theme of this picture is closely connected with the subject of the Last Judgment, a subject which appears early in the history of Netherlandish Art. Hieronymus Bosch also painted the Last Judgment in a vast triptych, probably the most important of all his altarpieces, painted for Philip the Fair in 1504. On the left wing of this work, representing Paradise, the Rebel Angels are seen in the clouds beneath the throne of God the Father, already in the form of monsters, cast down headlong by St. Michael with his angel hosts. The left wing of Bosch's so-called *Hay Cart* in the Escorial represents a similar subject. Brueghel himself treated the subject of the Last Judgment in a drawing of 1558 (Vienna, Albertina), a study for the engraving by Peter van der Heyden, still closely related in style to earlier artists, like Bosch. Even earlier, as we have seen in the picture of *St. Michael* (Plate 3), he painted the episode of the Fall of the Rebel Angels. Perhaps a recent treatment of this subject may have helped to sustain his interest in it. Frans Floris, the fashionable Antwerp painter of the day, painted in 1554 on the commission of the Armourers' Guild a great altarpiece dedicated to St. Michael (the central panel is today in the Antwerp Museum), for the Cathedral of his native city, a picture that certainly caused something of a sensation. In the excellently painted, if academically constructed, nudes, Floris appears, particularly in the representation of this subject, as the forerunner of Rubens. Brueghel — probably not unintentionally — produces something entirely different, something quite outside the general influences of the art of the day; in fact, although linking up with an older tradition, a thoroughly new and extremely original conception of the subject. While with Floris the main figure by no means stands out from the others, with Brueghel St. Michael is the central figure of the composition. His figure in glistening armour is slender, almost too fragile. It shows, for the first time in the whole of Brueghel's pictures, those over-long proportions which from the drawing of 1561, *Christ in Limbo*, onwards, became the rule for his idealized figures and constitute the chief characteristic of his own peculiar "mannerism" as a forerunner of Greco and the early Rubens. Here too St. Michael as the leader has hurried on in front of his companions and stands — as in that early picture he stands on earth — fighting single-handed among the bodies of the fantastically-formed, multitudinous rabble of Hell, that drifts down from the open Heavens in a long stream, followed and chased by a little band of Angels, fighting with swords and spears and blowing the trumpets of the Day of Judgment.

15.

TWO MONKEYS
Berlin, Kaiser Friedrich-Museum

On panel. 8 by 9 inches. Signed and dated lower left:
BRVEGEL · MDLXII
Two monkeys, fastened with chains, sit in the opening of
a window with a view over the Scheldt towards Antwerp.
It is impossible to decide whether a special meaning should
be attached to this picture, something in the sense of a
proverbial saying, or whether it is merely a work inspired
by chance in which the artist has immortalized two animals
which belonged to him. As the town in the background is undoubtedly Antwerp, of course Brueghel may have thought
of his dear fellow citizens rather in the same way as the
"Monkey of Heidelberg" which once adorned the bridge
over the Neckar as an emblem with the following verse:

> "Was thust du mich hier angaffen?
> hast du nicht gesehen den alten Affen?
> zu Heidelberg sieh dich hin u. her
> da findest du wohl meines gleichen mehr."

Translation:

> "What dost thou, gaping at me here?
> Hast thou not seen the old monkey?
> Look round about in Heidelberg
> There thou'lt surely find more of my kind."

16.

THE DEATH OF SAUL
Vienna, Kunsthistorisches Museum

On panel. 13 by 21 $^1/_2$ inches (at the top 1 $^1/_2$ inches, at the bottom $^1/_2$ inch are added). Signed lower left: BRVEGEL · M · CCCCC · LXII and besides the inscription: SAUL · XXXI · CAPIT.

In this very unusual subject, Brueghel has closely followed the Old Testament story in the 31st Chapter of the First Book of Samuel (cf. also I Chron. 11, I): "Now the Philistines fought against Israel: and the men of Israel fled from before the Philistines, and fell down slain in mount Gilboa. And the Philistines followed hard upon Saul and upon his sons: and the Philistines slew Jonathan, and Abinadab, and Melchishua, Saul's sons. And the battle went sore against Saul, and the archers hit him; and he was sore wounded of the archers. Then said Saul unto his armourbearer: Draw thy sword, and thrust me through therewith; lest these uncircumcised come and thrust me through, and abuse me. But his armourbearer would not; for he was sore afraid. Therefore Saul took a sword, and fell upon it. And when his armourbearer saw that Saul was dead, he fell likewise upon his sword, and died with him. So Saul died, and his three sons, and his armourbearer, and all his men, that same day together." In Brueghel's picture both armies are seen in the tumult of battle, on the right; on the left on a rocky hill lies Saul pierced by his own sword, and beside him the armourbearer, falling on his.

17.

LANDSCAPE
WITH THE FLIGHT INTO EGYPT
London, Collection of Count Antoine Seilern

On panel. 14 $\frac{1}{2}$ by 21 $\frac{3}{4}$ inches. Signed lower right: BRVEGEL . . .
D. L. XIII. This picture was only rediscovered in 1939 in the pro-
perty left by Mrs. Frank Holbrooke, Bladon Castle, Burton-on-
Trent, England. It was attributed to Brueghel by the writer when
the master's signature was still invisible under a heavy varnish, and
was purchased in the same year by the present owner, at a London
auction. This picture is evidently identical with the one recorded in
1607 in the collection of the Granvella family at Besançon, which
comprised also the property left by the Cardinal of the same name,
a warm friend of Brueghel's; probably the painting is identical with
one among Rubens' effects at his death.

The subject of the Flight into Egypt frequently occurs in German
paintings of the former half of the sixteenth century, and not
rarely in Netherlandish art where it was used by Brueghel's predecessors, Hieronymus Bosch and Joachim de Patinir. The subject was,
however, treated by these two masters in a way totally different
from Brueghel's, who created something thoroughly new and per-
sonal. He places the Holy Family on a hill in the foreground,
from where they turn into a wide landscape which dominates the
whole composition with its variety of rocks, trees, sheets of water,
and buildings. The magnificent conception of this landscape may
be considered a forerunner of the series of the Months (Plates 22
to 26), which Brueghel was to paint in 1565. The pictorial treatment, which appeals most to the eye, is considerably more deli-
cate than that of the Months, while being by no means less rich.

18.

THE TOWER OF BABEL
Vienna, Kunsthistorisches Museum

On panel. 45 by 61 inches. Signed on one of the quarry stones middle left:
BRVEGEL · FE · M · CCCCC · LXIII.

The subject of this picture occurs in French and Netherlandish painting of the 15th and 16th centuries. Many of Brueghel's contemporaries and a great number of his followers portrayed the same theme, evidently a very popular one, and Brueghel himself had used it already in a small picture on ivory, probably in 1553, which was in the estate of the miniaturist Giulio Clovio at his death, and has been lost since that time; and further in a small oil painting which probably was, just as the large one under discussion, in the collection of Emperor Rudolf II, and is probably identical with one in the collection of D. G. van Beuningen at Rotterdam. In the rendering of the various operations involved in the construction of the enormous building, Brueghel displays a particularly practical and technical interest in engineering. The reader may be reminded here that some years later he received a commission from the Brussels Town Council to paint a series of pictures of the excavation of the Canal between Brussels and Antwerp, a commission that, owing to the master's death, was never executed. The view of the town with its sea of houses spreading out behind the mighty building and the distant aqueduct reminds us of the background of that earlier picture of *Christ driving the Money Changers out of the Temple* (Plate 5) in which, however, the magnificence of the spacious view is not yet attained. In the foreground on the left, surrounded by his attendants and architects, is seen the builder himself, a king who may be recognized as Nimrod.

With the confusion of tongues, Brueghel's tower probably has little to do; it represents for him more a symbol of the perverse World, rather in the sense of Brant's "Ship of Fools":

> "Nemroth wolt buwen hoch jn lufft
> Eyn grossen thurn für wassers klüfft,
> Und schlůg nit an das jm zů swår
> Sin buwen vnd nit mőglich wår,"

where he suggests that Nimrod, when he attempted to build the Tower of Babel, had not taken into account the vanity and insufficiency of human actions.

19.

CHRIST CARRYING THE CROSS
Vienna, Kunsthistorisches Museum

On panel. 49 by 67 inches. Signed lower right: B R V E G E L MD · LXIIII.
Brueghel's conception of this scene of the Passion, represented without regard
for chronological accuracy of detail, simply as an execution in the dress of his
own times, can be traced to earlier examples, dating back as far as the times of
the Van Eyck. His own immediate forerunner is the original artist Jan van Amstel,
called "de Hollander", or the "Brunswick Monogrammist", and we find Herri
met de Bles and Pieter Aertsen working on the same lines. But here too Brueghel
goes further than his predecessors and treats the subject as a comprehensive picture
of human life. In a wide, sunny and hilly landscape innumerable people are moving,
tempted out of doors by the prospect of the spectacle of a public execution. In the
middle distance, a procession makes its way through the crowd, accompanied by
red-coated soldiers who conduct the condemned to the place of execution, a hill
of moderate height on the right of the picture with gallows and wheels. Only after
a close inspection one discovers in the middle of the long procession, and in the
very middle of the picture, the chief figure, the Saviour collapsing under the weight
of the cross. Further on in the procession the two thieves, accompanied by a priest,
are drawn along in a one-horse cart. Everyone is hastening towards the scene of
execution, around which a circle of eager spectators has already formed. The rest
of the populace among whom are to be seen many women and children, streams
out of the town in the background and hurries in the same direction, thronging
and pushing, called to order here and there by the numerous soldiers; but they
are all in a holiday mood, light-hearted and insensitive; they take little part
in the sad proceedings; they are out for entertainment and pleasure, not sorrow
and certainly not edification. It is the topsy-turvy World which does not even
trouble itself about its Lord. In strong contrast is the group of real mourners,
who have withdrawn by themselves to a low rocky hill in the foreground on
the right. Mary has completely broken down and is supported by St. John the
Evangelist and surrounded by the mourning figures of the holy women. These
figures have nothing in common with the extremely realistic forms of the others.
With their elongated proportions and their robes of purposely undatable style, they
show the type that Brueghel, as we have seen, reserved for his ideal characters.

20.

THE DEATH OF THE VIRGIN (GRISAILLE)
London, National Gallery

On panel. 14 by 21 inches. Signed lower right: BRVEGEL, and below signs of a date no longer legible.

Brueghel painted this little picture for his friend, the famous Netherlandish geographer Abraham Ortelius (1522—1598), who had it engraved, no doubt with the artist's approval, for himself and his friends by Philips Galle. The verses accompanying the engraving were intended not only for his patron, but also for Brueghel himself. We give them in translation: "As Thou, Blessed Virgin, longedst for the reign of Thy beloved Son, what joys filled Thy Breast! What seemed sweeter to Thee than to leave this earthly prison and travel towards the high Temple of the much desired Kingdom! As Thou didst leave the holy company, whose patron Thou hadst been, how sadly and at the same time how happily Thy Son's and Thy own disciples saw Thee departing! What was more comforting to them than that Thou didst reign, what sadder than that they should be denied the light of Thy presence! The joyful attitude of the righteous, and their air of melancholy are shown in this picture from a master's hand."

With this subject Brueghel pays his tribute of veneration to the Virgin Mary. This is shown not only by the contents of the verses quoted above, but also by the passionate interest in the scene, already a favourite with Netherlandish artists before him. The number of mourners is no longer limited to the twelve apostles, but a thronging crowd of more than thirty spectators surrounds the sick-bed of the dying woman. In the foreground, to the right, a monk is ringing the death-bell. A female figure, obviously St. Mary Magdalen, smoothes the pillows, an old, grey-bearded man, no doubt St. Peter, hands her the lighted candle of the dying. Opposite, in the foreground on the left, is seated a young man whom we believe to be St. John the Evangelist who, worn out with sick-nursing and night-vigils, has sunk down by the fireplace, unaware that the Mother of God, whom he so deeply worships, is at the hour of death. A fine trait this, revealing the bitter irony of Life and Fate, such as Brueghel delighted in. The soft half-light so skilfully produced by the modest means of the monochrome technique foreshadows Rembrandt. It is the only grisaille painting left to us from Brueghel's hand; he is known to have painted several and no doubt they inspired Rubens and Van Dyck in the grisaille studies for engravings carried out in their workshops.

21.

THE ADORATION OF THE MAGI
London, National Gallery

On panel. 42 $\frac{1}{2}$ by 32 $\frac{1}{2}$ inches. Signed and dated lower right:

BRVEGEL. MD · LXIIII.

This picture differs in every way from the early version of the same subject in the Brussels Gallery (Plate 6); the comparatively few figures and the upright, narrow shape of the picture are most unusual for Brueghel. These peculiarities cannot be attributed to any direct commission or order. It seems much more probable to us that it was the artist's own choice for once in a way to try another form for his composition; furthermore, it reveals the direction in which the artist's style was tending to develop. As Georges Hulin de Loo has observed with rare perception, we find here for the first time in a picture of Brueghel's, the inclination towards a more concentrated treatment of the subject, rather in the manner of compositions such as *Christ and the Adulteress*, *The Death of the Virgin* (Plate 20), and *The Resurrection*, all apparently grisailles, only one of which has survived. The National Gallery picture in particular has the upright, narrow shape in common with *The Resurrection*, and both works, with their lively yet closely shut-in plan of composition and the overlong proportions which we first find in the *Fall of the Rebel Angels* (Plate 14) of the year 1562, in the Brussels Museum, seem to show decisively that Brueghel was not altogether uninfluenced by the Italian mannerists of his time such as Parmigianino. In spite of the comparatively calm tempo of the composition, reminding one almost of the "Sante conversazioni", "Brueghel's picture is entirely un-Italian in spirit, chiefly on account of the extremely un-Italian conception of the proceedings." "In the rendering of the psychological moment", continues Max Dvořák, who has written the best and most conclusive description of this picture, "lies, perhaps, the picture's most remarkable characteristic. The key note is the awkward stare of dull astonishment. But these gapes are allied to a higher feeling; a shy sense of solemnity, a half-unconscious devotion, which is expressed more in the general stillness and unaccustomed silence than in gestures or violent emotions; simple people behave in church on Sunday in a similar way. This mass feeling appears too in the demeanour of the Three Holy Kings, different only in degree as they seem to be the spokesmen. They are diametrically removed from all pathos, from every heroic pose and subjective emphasis. Their adoration is awkward and clumsy; one could laugh at it, if only this rude, primitive feeling had not in it so much that is true and convincing."

22.

THE HUNTERS IN THE SNOW
Vienna, Kunsthistorisches Museum

On panel. 46 by 63³/₄ inches. Signed and dated lower centre:
BRVEGEL · M · D · LXV.

This picture obviously belongs to the same series as the four reproduced in the following plates. It is generally assumed that these five
pictures represent an incomplete series of the Months. In 1594, a series
of six pictures was presented by the city of Antwerp to Archduke Ernest
of Austria, who was then Stadholder of the Netherlands. Probably they
were the five pictures under discussion, together with a sixth one that
has been lost since. According to the calendar then in use, the series
would have to begin with March/April (Plate 23). The missing painting would, therefore, have to represent the months of November and
December.

In this Winter Landscape, with the lowering grey sky, the dark silhou-
ettes of the hunters, the hounds, the trees and the crows, outlined
against the white of the snow, with some country people boiling something at an open fire in front of the inn at the sign of the Stag, with the
deep grey expanse of frozen water on which skaters are disporting
themselves in the distance, we think we may recognize February. This
is the month to which, in the Calendar pictures of illuminated manuscripts, as for instance in the prayer-book of the Duc de Berry at Chan-
tilly of the beginning of the 15th century and the Breviarium Grimani
at Venice of the beginning of the 16th century, the snow-landscape
belongs. If we may presume that each picture represents two months,
the painting under consideration would comprise January and February.

23.

THE STORMY DAY
Vienna, Kunsthistorisches Museum

On panel. 46 $^1/_2$ by 64 inches. Signed and dated lower left: BRVEGEL MDLXV. Cf. our remarks on Plate 22.

In this gloomy landscape with the cloudy, overcast sky, and the snowy mountains, the stormy sea in which ships are battling, the bare trees lead one to imagine a picture of earliest spring; perhaps the month of March is intended. If we presume that each picture represents two months, the painting under consideration will comprise March and April.

24.

THE HAY HARVEST
Raudnitz, Collection of Fürst Lobkowitz

On panel, 45 by 62 $^1/_4$ inches. Unsigned. Cf. our remarks on Plate 22.

In the middle distance, in the whole breadth of the picture, hay is harvested; in a long, straggling meadow it is gathered into haycocks and piled onto a wagon. On the left a peasant sharpens his scythe, three peasant women stride along with their wooden rakes; on the right men and women take away vegetables and fruit, cherries among them, some in a cart, some in baskets, which they carry on their heads to the neighbouring village. Probably this is June, the month of the Hay Harvest. If two months are intended, they will be May and June.

25.

THE CORN HARVEST
New York, Metropolitan Museum of Art

On panel. 46 by 63 inches. Signed lower right: BRVEGEL, and below the remains of a date of which only the last letters .... LXV are still legible. Cf. our remarks on Plate 22.

It is the hour of the midday siesta and only a few people are still busy reaping and binding the sheaves. Country people of both sexes are resting under the shadow of a tree and refreshing themselves with bread, milk and water; one peasant is already enjoying his midday slumber, another comes up a path deeply cut through the standing corn bringing a jug of fresh drink. The picture seems to represent the month of July, the time of reaping corn. If two months are intended, they will be July and August.

26.

THE RETURN OF THE HERD
Vienna, Kunsthistorisches Museum

On panel. 46 by 62 $^1/_2$ inches. Signed and dated lower left: BRVEGEL MDLXV. Cf. our remarks on Plate 22. The cattle are driven back to their village home with poles by the herdsmen whose leader is mounted on a pony. In the middle distance is seen a birdcatcher's net, on the hillsides, leading down to the river, a vineyard in which men are at work, and nearby — no doubt intended by Brueghel as an ironical touch — a place of execution with gallows and wheels. The cold air and the cutting wind which seems to come towards us out of the luminous atmosphere of the picture, the leafless trees, as well as the cattle returning home and the work in the vineyard all point to late Autumn; the month of November has been generally accepted as the subject of this picture, but the month of October could also be intended. If we assume that each picture represents two months, they will be September and October.

27.

THE WEDDING DANCE IN THE OPEN AIR
Detroit, Institute of Art

On panel. 47 by 62 inches. Dated lower right: · M · D · LXVI. The picture has suffered from rubbing and repainting. First published by Wilhelm K. Valentiner.

In this picture the Bride who has already left her seat, still distinguishable by the crown suspended over it, has joined the dancers and is to be recognized in the young woman rather in the middle of the composition who wears a wreath-like head-dress, not the white coif of the other peasant women. Whether her partner is the Bridegroom is another question; he usually plays a small part in Brueghel's wedding scenes and is not generally to be identified with certainty. In the profusion of the composition and in the arrangement of the numerous persons and groups of the lively feast, the Detroit picture surpasses the earlier versions of the same theme and without doubt represents it in its final form. In the similar pictures of the *Peasants' Wedding* and the *Dance of the Peasants* (Plates 42 and 43), in the Kunsthistorisches Museum in Vienna, Brueghel achieves, at the end of his life, a still more intensive simplification and coherence.

28.

THE NUMBERING OF THE PEOPLE
AT BETHLEHEM
Brussels, Royal Museum

On panel. 46 by 64 ³/₄ inches. Signed and dated lower right:
BRVEGEL 1566.

The subject of this picture is hardly known in the history of pictorial art before Brueghel, but, according to Georges Hulin de Loo, probably occurs in the Mystery Plays and is taken from the beginning of the second chapter of the Gospel according to St. Luke: "And it came to pass in those days, that there went out a decree from Caesar Augustus, that all the world should be taxed. (And this taxing was first made when Cyrenius was governor of Syria.) And all went to be taxed, everyone into his own city. And Joseph also went up from Galilee, out of the city of Nazareth into Judæa, unto the city of David, which is called Bethlehem (because he was of the house and lineage of David), to be taxed with Mary his espoused wife, being great with child". It was evidently a proclamation for the purpose of a census and at the same time for the assessment and levy of a tax. To Brueghel, Bethlehem is a Netherlandish village in the usual bustle of winter affairs: the inhabitants are busy with killing pigs, carrying wood, sweeping up the snow and similar occupations. The children who here again play an important part, throw snowballs, skate and slide on the ice, spin tops and so on. The official Commission have made their headquarters in an inn at the sign of the Green Wreath on the left, and are established with their books and papers; and here, as though it were a conscription of soldiers in our own day, the people are crowding up for registration. St. Joseph makes his way towards them past wagons laden with casks, leading the ox and the ass on which Mary is seated, warmly wrapped up and in need of protection; soon Joseph too will join the ranks of those presenting themselves for registration.

29.

THE MASSACRE OF THE HOLY INNOCENTS
Vienna, Kunsthistorisches Museum

On panel. 43³/₄ by 63 inches. Signed lower right: BRVEG...
We meet with this subject in the history of art before Brueghel's
day; but there is no doubt that it is a conceit of his own that,
as an excuse for introducing his own country people and their surroundings, he not only dresses the peasants and soldiers in the
costumes of his own times, but also goes a step further and lays
the scene in the setting of a Netherlandish village in winter. For
him, as a Northerner, Christmas Time means frost and snow and
so, without further consideration, the Gospel subjects of the
Numbering of the People (Plate 28), the *Massacre of the Holy
Innocents*, the *Adoration of the Magi* (Plate 32) take place in the
cold of the Netherlandish winter. Whether the *Numbering of the
People* and the *Massacre of the Holy Innocents* can be thought of
as companion pieces is uncertain, as with Brueghel the fact that
pictures are of the same dimensions is not of much significance;
besides, both subjects are taken from the accounts in the Gospels
of St. Matthew and St. Luke which almost repeat themselves. Was
Brueghel thinking in the *Massacre of the Holy Innocents* of the
bloody deeds of the Spanish "soldatesca" in his own country? The
form of the sinister Commander as the rider with the coat of arms
suggests to the modern spectator the Duke of Alba, so often
represented in ferocious guise, but who, if we are right in dating the
picture 1566, only made his entry into the Netherlands a year later.

30.

ST. JOHN THE BAPTIST PREACHING REPENTANCE
Budapest, Museum of Fine Arts. Lent by the Batthyány family

On panel. 37 ½ by 63 inches. Signed and dated lower right:

BRVEGEL · M · D · LXVI.

The subject in question frequently occurs in Netherlandish painting
from the beginning of the sixteenth century onwards, for instance in
the work of one of Brueghel's immediate predecessors, the landscape
painter Herri met de Bles. Its fullest development, however, is first
to be found in the work of Brueghel himself, who may have been inspired in particular by the very popular open-air sermons held among
the reformed religious communities which were so numerous in his own
day. In his History of the Decline of the United Netherlands through
the Spanish government, Schiller devotes a chapter to this open-air
preaching which he describes with great intuitive perception. Men and
women, the latter often accompanied by quite small children, of all
classes and ranks flocked from all sides to these gatherings. "A great
many were attracted by this preaching as by an amusing comedy, in
which the Pope, the Fathers of the Congress of Trent, Purgatory and
other dogmas of the ruling church were abused in a droll way. The
madder this drollery became, the more were ears tickled, and a general
clapping of hands, as in a theatre, rewarded the Preacher who most sur-
passed the others in adventurous exaggeration." In a similar way
Brueghel, without expressing any criticism, lets the Baptist appear in
the midst of a similar chance assembly of attentive humanity composed in a very picturesque way of citizens, labourers, peasants, gipsies
of both sexes, and monks, one of whom, as a member of the Brother-
hood of St. Anthony, even wears a T embroidered on his grey habit.
Boys climb trees in order to hear better. Among those present, only
one of the listeners strikes one as belonging to a more exalted rank,
in the fashionable dress of the day: the man who, rather in the
centre of the composition, is having his hand read by a gipsy. It
is the only real portrait-head in the whole picture. Might Brueghel
here in jest have portrayed one of his friends, such, for instance, as the
Nuremberg merchant, Hans Franckert, who, according to Van Mander,
loved to mingle secretly with the people in Brueghel's company?

31.

WINTER LANDSCAPE
WITH SKATERS AND BIRDTRAP
Brussels, Collection of Dr. F. Delporte

On panel. 15 by 22 inches. Signed and dated lower right:
BRVEGEL · M · D · LXV.
Beside the pictures of winter with Bible subjects (Plates 28, 29, 32)
and that from the series of the Months (Plate 22), the composition
in question, the grandiose design of which seems to extend far
beyond the small dimensions of the picture, as a pure landscape,
plays a not unimportant rôle in Brueghel's work; for according
to records and existing drawings and engravings, he probably
painted a large number of pure landscapes. Whether the birdtrap
to be seen on the right of the picture has also still further the
special significance of a proverb, of course we cannot say for
certain. It is possible that Brueghel may have meant to imply
that security of life is not granted even to the birds of the air,
even as on earth the skaters on the ice may typify the pre-
cariousness of existence. However that may be, with this picture
Brueghel appears as an unrivalled forerunner of Dutch seventeenth century art, in which the Winter landscape reaches
great eminence as a particularly favourite class of painting.

32.

THE ADORATION OF THE MAGI IN THE SNOW
Winterthur, Collection of Oskar Reinhart

On panel. 13¾ by 21¾ inches. Lower left a very faint inscription which we believe can be read as follows: M · D · LXVII BRVEGEL. In this little picture Brueghel sets a sacred subject in the wintry atmos= phere of a homely little village, and his imagination here strikes the same note as Altdorfer's who, in his famous composition of the *Nativity*, in the Vienna Gallery, which Brueghel is hardly likely to have known, surrounded the Holy Night with all the poetry of a snow-landscape. Appropriately enough, the village of Bethlehem looks exactly as it does in the pictures of the *Numbering of the People* and the *Massacre of the Holy Innocents*. The three Holy Kings have found the Mother and the Babe in the snow-covered, tumble-down shed and pay their homage there. Their train, to which the soldiers seen through a gap in the distance between two houses also belong, is smaller than in the earlier picture in tempera of the same subject in the Brussels Museum (Plate 6), larger however than in the upright picture in the National Gallery in London (Plate 21). In addition, the life and doings of the village in our picture proceed undisturbed, and the inhabi- tants do not appear to bother themselves much about the unaccustomed visitors. The genre interest here completely stifles the Gospel story. Once again Brueghel has set himself a completely new problem that is entirely different from his earlier versions of the same subject. The heavy snowstorm that envelops the whole village and the busy people is most remarkable. This too is a new idea of Brueghel's and one that is almost unknown in the History of Art before him. The same charming effect was rendered again in the beautiful *Village in Winter*, of the year 1586, in the Vienna Gallery, by Lucas van Valckenborch, to whom the invention of this motive had been attributed. As is now shown, it belongs to a much greater genius.

33.

THE CONVERSION OF ST. PAUL
Vienna, Kunsthistorisches Museum

On panel. 42 $^1/_2$ by 61 $^1/_2$ inches. Signed and dated lower right:
BRVEGEL · M · D · LXVII.

The subject matter of this picture was not unknown to earlier
Netherlandish Art; we need only think, for example, of an
engraving by Lucas van Leyden and of a picture by Jean Belle-
gambe. Again Brueghel interprets it in an entirely new way, by
making of the chief subject nothing less than an army crossing the
Alps, an idea which may have been suggested to him by the Duke
of Alba who in exactly the same year, 1567, crossed the Alps of
Savoy with his Spanish troops to bring captivity to the Netherlands. The chief figure, Saul (who of course has nothing to do
with the inflexible Alba who became no Paul), is seen here just as
in the *Carrying of the Cross* (Plate 19) far back in the middle of
the composition, thrown from his horse, according to the words
of the Acts of the Apostles (9, 3): "And as he journeyed, he came
near Damascus, and suddenly there shined round about him a
light from Heaven, and he fell to the earth, and heard a voice
saying unto him: Saul, Saul, why persecutest thou me? And he
said: Who art thou, Lord? And the Lord said: I am Jesus whom
thou persecutest, it is hard for thee to kick against the pricks."

34.

FOOLS' PARADISE
Munich, Ältere Pinakothek

On panel. 20½ by 30¾ inches. Signed and dated lower left:
M · DLXVII · BRVEGEL.

Under a tree with a round table encircling it on which all sorts of
delicacies are placed in readiness, lie sluggards of three degrees of
social standing: the Peasant, the Soldier, the Writer, sprawling at
ease, exhausted by the pleasures of the table. The fences are made
of sausages. From under the roof of a pent-house on which tarts are
growing (see Plate 10, No. 1) a knight looks out, while a roasted
fowl flies into his open mouth; an opened egg walks by on two
legs; a roasted fowl lies ready on a plate; a roasted pig runs about
with a knife stuck in his side; a cactus-like plant appears to be
made of cakes. In the background a man with a spoon is eating
his way through a mountain of butter.

Many motives, like the tarts on the roof and the mountain of butter,
occur in German fairy tales; for instance, in the tale of "Hänsel
und Gretel". As the idea of the Fools' Paradise is common to almost
all the countries of Europe and is to be met with in Hans Sachs and
Fischart, a closer comparison along these lines would lead us too
far afield. It appears essentially to belong to the class of those tales
of exaggeration and mendacity among which its unlikelihoods and
impossibilities seem to place it. But did Brueghel mean to imply no
more than that by it? Perhaps he was playing with the idea of a sort
of Utopia of general well-being, such as the political and religious
upheavals of his day might have led many people to hope for.

35.

THE FAITHLESSNESS OF THE WORLD
Naples, Museo Nazionale

Tempera on canvas. 34 by 33 $\frac{1}{2}$ inches. Signed and dated in the left corner of the frame: BRVEGEL 1568. Under the subject is the inscription:

> "Om dat de Werelt is soe ongetru
> Daer om gha ic in den ru"

That means: "As the world is so untrue, I go in mourning." The old grey-bearded man, disillusioned by the World, paces sadly along, threatened by the caltrops before him on the ground and at his back the symbolical figure of the World cutting his purse. We have already met this strained, crouching figure in the glass orb in Brueghel's picture of the Proverbs in Berlin (Plate 10, No. 43) and it has here too the secondary proverbial meaning: "One must bend in order to go through the World". It is the upright who are doomed to mourn.

36.

THE PROVERB OF THE BIRD'S NEST
Vienna, Kunsthistorisches Museum

On panel. 23 $\frac{1}{4}$ by 26 $\frac{3}{4}$ inches. Signed and dated lower left:
BRVEGEL MD · LXVIII.
Georges Hulin de Loo has found the right interpretation
for the subject of this picture in a Netherlandish proverb:
"Dije de nest weet, dije weeten, dijen rooft, dije heeten,"
which means roughly: "He who knows where the nest is
has the knowledge, he who steals it has the nest." According
to this, the Peasant is not threatening the boy with his left
hand, but only pointing towards the nest, the position of
which he knows, while the boy climbs the tree without his
knowledge and robs the nest. This would well accord with
Brueghel's ideas on the subject of the perversity of the World.
Sebastian Brant interprets the stealing of a nest somewhat
differently as the symbol of self-will and arrogance:

> "Wer off syn eygnen synn vszflügt,
> Der selb zûn vogel nâster stygt,
> Das er offt vff der erden lygt,"

commenting on the obstinacy of people who hunt for birds'
nests, but, as an old proverb has it, the higher they climb,
the further they fall.

37.

THE CRIPPLES
Paris, Louvre

On panel. 7 by 8¹/₄ inches. Signed and dated lower left:
BRVEGEL · M · D · LXVIII.

The strange subject of this picture would seem less remarkable to
Brueghel's contemporaries, who still found an interest in bodily
deformities and indeed really delighted in Court Fools and Dwarfs,
than it does in our own hypocritical, soft-hearted times. In his
early picture of *Christ driving the money changers out of the Temple*
(Plate 5), Brueghel painted a pair of such cripples with powerful
realism, and in the picture of the *Battle between Carnival and
Lent* (Plate 9), we already find a whole group similar to that in
this little picture, the tone of which is indicated by Max Dvořák
with fine perception: "As though a family of poisonous toad-
stools had sprung up in a lonely corner out of the dark earth."
What Brueghel meant by this subject is not quite clear. The
supposition of R. van Bastelaer that these Beggars ("Gueux")
might be taken as an allusion to the political party of the Geuse
which was attacking Granvella, the Stadholder, is not to be
lightly dismissed. The emblems of this party were the fox-tails
which with *one* exception the cripples are wearing. Of course in
the year 1568 the power of the Geuse had long been broken.

38.

THE MERRY WAY TO THE GALLOWS
Darmstadt, Museum

On panel. 18 by 20 inches. Signed and dated left: BRVEGEL · 1568.
The explanation of Van Mander according to which the magpie
perching on the gallows represents a talebearer or gossip deemed
fit for the gallows is much too artificial to be to the point. Furthermore, there is not only *one* magpie to be seen in the picture, for
a second one perches on the rock at the foot of the gallows with
which it seems to have nothing at all to do. The meaning of the
subject is actually fairly clear. A straggling procession of peasant
men and women streams up from the village below to the hill on
which the gallows stand. The people are in a gay mood and a
bagpiper comes with them. Three dancers have come by chance, as it
seems, quite unconsciously close to the place of execution. Two men
stand on the left, one of whom points with his hands to the gallows
and perhaps calls out to the dancers to remind them that this is not
exactly a seemly place for their merriment. Now there is in
fact a German proverb that exactly suits the circumstances: "Der
Galgenweg geht auch durch lustige Auen" (The way to the Gallows
leads through pleasant meadows) and which is expressed more
concisely in the Netherlandish saying "aan de galg dansen". It is the
contrast between the folly of mankind and the beauty of nature that
entirely expresses Brueghel's conception of the World and Man.

39.

THE PARABLE OF THE BLIND
Naples, Museo Nazionale

Tempera on canvas. 34 by 60 $^1/_2$ inches. Signed and dated lower left:
BRVEGEL · M · D · LX · VIII.
The parable of the blind, as is well known, comes from the Gospel:
"Let them alone: they be blind leaders of the blind. And if the blind
lead the blind, both shall fall into the ditch". At the beginning of the
16th century, the idea was familiar among the current conceptions of
that time, as we are reminded by Sebastian Brant when he says in the
Ship of Fools:

"Eyn blindt den andern schyltet blindt,
Wie wol sie beid gefallen synt."
(Two blind men who have fallen into a ditch
reproach each other with blindness.)

In the history of Netherlandish painting the subject might have been
introduced by Hieronymus Bosch in a picture that still closely follows
the Bible by restricting the number of blind men to *two*. Cornelis Metsys
first makes of it a procession of *four* blind men walking in single file.
Brueghel has *six* of them arranged diagonally across the picture-plane:
the foremost has already fallen into the water, the next threatens soon
to follow him, and on him depend the four others who, with long poles
and hands on each others' shoulders follow tentatively, destined to share
the same fate.
What did Brueghel mean by this sublime creation? The fact that he
has introduced a larger number of the unfortunate blind men than
any of his predecessors no doubt implies that there was a concrete
idea behind it; probably he was thinking of one of those wandering
preachers who, in his day, risen from the lowest classes, or at most
from the artisan class, so often succeeded in attracting great crowds
of followers of certain sects, thus becoming the ignorant leader of
an ignorant multitude. Religious as Brueghel was himself, he did
not see in such preachers true faith but rather blind superstition. He
remains here fundamentally faithful to the spirit of the gospel parable.

40.

THE UNFAITHFUL SHEPHERD
Philadelphia, Museum, Collection of John G. Johnson

On panel. 24 by 33 $^1/_2$ inches. Much repainted, therefore scarcely to be thought of as original, although no doubt the composition was originally Brueghel's.

Brueghel has represented the Parable of the Good Shepherd in a wonderful drawing, dated 1565, engraved by Philips Galle. In this drawing in the background on either side two scenes are introduced, one of which shows the good shepherd struggling with the wolf, the other, the unfaithful shepherd fleeing from the wolf, according to the words of the Gospel according to St. John: "I am the good shepherd: the good shepherd giveth his life for the sheep. But he that is an hireling, and not the shepherd, whose own the sheep are not, seeth the wolf coming, and leaveth the sheep and fleeth: and the wolf catcheth them, and scattereth the sheep." This shepherd who is no shepherd is represented in Brueghel's picture. He runs swiftly home along a forked path and leaves his sheep like a coward to the wolf, which has already caught one of the unfortunate animals, while the others try to escape.

41.

HEAD OF AN OLD PEASANT WOMAN
Munich, Ältere Pinakothek

On panel. 8 ³/₄ by 7 inches. Unsigned.

Portraits by Brueghel are no longer preserved, or at least
they have disappeared and are unknown. Of the studies of
heads which he must no doubt have painted but which, like
his drawings from nature, he did not repeat exactly in his
pictures, we know only this one which we think may be
dated about the time of the following pictures of the *Dance
of the Peasants* and the *Peasants' Wedding* (Pl. 43 and 42).

42.

THE PEASANTS' WEDDING
Vienna, Kunsthistorisches Museum

On panel. 45 by 64 inches (a strip of about 2 inches has been added below). No signature is now visible.

The festive company is seated at a long table placed obliquely across the picture-plane. The guests do not exceed 20, the number prescribed by Charles V in a proclamation as the limit for participators in country weddings such as this. In the middle, beneath a crown suspended over her head, is seated the hideous Bride in the apathetic and indifferent attitude which from that time became conventional in Netherlandish painting. As in the *Wedding Dance* (Plate 27), the figure of the Bridegroom, on the other hand, is not rendered unmistakably conspicuous; should it be the man eating so eagerly on the left, two places away from the Bride? Who the citizen may be in black with hat and sword, with whom a Franciscan Friar at the right end of the table is apparently eagerly interceding, is not clear to us; some have thought of the painter himself who, according to Van Mander, took part in such feasts, of course in peasant dress. His features, however, judging by the engraved portrait, look different; perhaps he is the Lord of the Manor, or the Judge or the village magistrate. Dishes are carried by two peasant boys on the unhinged door of a barn; a third boy pours out wine; two bagpipers make music; a little girl seated on the ground is indulging in the pleasures of the table, and in the background on the left a closely thronging, inquisitive crowd is seen pouring in through an open door.

43.

THE DANCE OF THE PEASANTS
Vienna, Kunsthistorisches Museum

On panel. 45 by 64 $^1/_2$ inches. Signed lower right: BRVEGEL. The work under consideration is related, as we have seen, to Brueghel's earlier subjects of Wedding Dances, and with it the subject reaches its greatest perfection. The number of figures is substantially reduced, their size much increased. The Bride and the table with presents are entirely absent and with them the connection with the Wedding-feast. The atmosphere here seems to have increased in warmth compared with the comparative coldness of the Feast. Look, for example, at the lively group of topers on the left; the pair of lovers kissing behind them; the bagpiper playing with full cheeks and real fervour, while a young peasant listens devotedly; the dancing couples on the right, among them an old couple in the foreground with their backs turned to the spectator; the onlookers in the background among whom a peasant in the motley dress of a Fool seems to strike the right note. In the foreground on the left a little girl and another still younger are imitating the dance-movements of their elders. Axel L. Romdahl is here reminded of the proverb, that after Brueghel's day was so often rendered by Jordaens and Steen: "Soo de ouden songen, soo pypen de jongen" (As the old folks sing, the young folks pipe).

44.

THE SEASCAPE
Vienna, Kunsthistorisches Museum

On panel. 27³/₄ by 38 inches. Unsigned.

A partiality for the sea is shown early in Netherlandish painting. In the lives of coast-dwellers the sea, as the source of their well-being, plays an especially important and valuable part.

After the earlier representations of the sea in miniatures and pictures as a background to the subject, we finally meet true marine pieces among the paintings on linen in the possession of the Medici, in the fifteenth century, of which of course not the least trace remains. In the 16th century we find a picture of a stormy sea painted by Herri met de Bles among a series of landscapes in the Naples Museum, of course only very inadequately realized. From the beginning of his career, Brueghel's mind was constantly occupied with the sea: we need only recall the *"Harbour at Naples"* (Plate 1), the *Sea Battle of Messina* engraved by Frans Huys, and the series of ships reproduced by this engraver and others. The picture under consideration is of exceptional excellence; it is today generally recognized as a work of Brueghel's and unanimously placed among the master's latest works. It may be considered as the earliest example of Netherlandish marine painting. Max J. Friedländer thinks that possibly a proverb is illustrated here. This supposition seems to us to be a certainty, according to the following information for which we have to thank Dr. Ludwig Burchard: "Fleeing Ship, Whale and Barrel (between the two); these three elements make an emblem the meaning of which is given in the following passage from Zedlers Universal Lexicon (1732—1750): 'When the Whale plays with the barrel thrown in front of him and gives the ship time to escape, it is the picture of one who wastes his time and sacrifices his true well-being in pursuit of trifling things.' And it is just as clear that the barrel which is sacrificed contains the most valuable possession that the crew have on board, fresh water, which will be thrown 'into the jaws of the menacing enemy.'" It is to be hoped that proof in confirmation of this doubtless relevant explanation will be found to exist in 16th century sources.

LIST OF PLATES

1. THE HARBOUR AT NAPLES
2. LANDSCAPE WITH MARTYRDOM OF ST. CATHERINE
3. THE ARCHANGEL MICHAEL
4. LANDSCAPE WITH THE TEMPTATION OF ST. ANTHONY
5. CHRIST DRIVING THE MONEY CHANGERS OUT OF THE TEMPLE
6. THE ADORATION OF THE MAGI (IN TEMPERA)
7. RIVER LANDSCAPE WITH THE PEASANT SOWING
8. LANDSCAPE WITH THE FALL OF ICARUS
9. THE BATTLE BETWEEN CARNIVAL AND LENT
10. THE NETHERLANDISH PROVERBS
11. CHILDREN'S GAMES
12. THE TRIUMPH OF DEATH
13. MAD MEG («DULLE GRIET»)
14. THE FALL OF THE REBEL ANGELS
15. TWO MONKEYS
16. THE DEATH OF SAUL
17. LANDSCAPE WITH THE FLIGHT INTO EGYPT
18. THE TOWER OF BABEL
19. CHRIST CARRYING THE CROSS
20. THE DEATH OF THE VIRGIN (GRISAILLE)
21. THE ADORATION OF THE MAGI
22. THE HUNTERS IN THE SNOW
23. THE STORMY DAY
24. THE HAY HARVEST
25. THE CORN HARVEST
26. THE RETURN OF THE HERD
27. THE WEDDING DANCE IN THE OPEN AIR
28. THE NUMBERING OF THE PEOPLE AT BETHLEHEM
29. THE MASSACRE OF THE HOLY INNOCENTS
30. ST. JOHN THE BAPTIST PREACHING REPENTANCE
31. WINTER LANDSCAPE WITH SKATERS AND BIRDTRAP
32. THE ADORATION OF THE MAGI IN THE SNOW
33. THE CONVERSION OF ST. PAUL
34. FOOLS' PARADISE
35. THE FAITHLESSNESS OF THE WORLD
36. THE PROVERB OF THE BIRD'S NEST
37. THE CRIPPLES
38. THE MERRY WAY TO THE GALLOWS
39. THE PARABLE OF THE BLIND
40. THE UNFAITHFUL SHEPHERD
41. HEAD OF AN OLD PEASANT WOMAN
42. THE PEASANTS' WEDDING
43. THE DANCE OF THE PEASANTS
44. THE SEASCAPE